The Butterfly Series

Maria Ramos-Chertok

ADVANCE PRAISE FOR *The Butterfly Series*

"Moving from change to transformation requires both discipline and freedom. Whether you are looking for healing or motivation, *The Butterfly Series* offers you insightful next steps while honoring your past, present, and future."
—Ann Salerno, author of *The Change Cycle*

"Praise for Maria Ramos-Chertok's Butterfly Series I and II. A creative and practical approach to inspire self-reflection and goal setting through writing and art. The weekly writing prompts have given me an opportunity to turn one subject over and over and peel back the layers of inquiry to deepen my understanding. The workshop's combination of left and right brain activities was a perfect way for me to look at trauma, healing, and to set my intention on how I would take flight next."
—Claudine Naganuma,
Director of dNaga, Danspace and GIRL Project

"*The Butterfly Series* is like candy to personal development nerds like me! It's like turning to a friend for advice—and one that is available right away! When I feel stuck, I pull it from my drawer, and it's the dose of tough love I need. The writing prompts tap into some deep truths, like admitting I want to be a martial artist; or visioning out what I need, like finding my dream apartment! Feeling in flux with loved ones, with life purpose, or with anything, isn't easy and *The Butterfly Series* taught me to be present to the changes—with an open heart to the unknown and to my potential."

—Virada Chatikul, Tai Chi instructor and creative entrepreneur

"I am so thankful for *The Butterfly Series*. It both names the burdens womxn carry, and offers a framework for moving through them from a place of power."

—Janine Macbeth, artist, author, and publisher of Blood Orange Press

The Butterfly Series

Fifty-Two Weeks of Inquiries for Transformation

Maria Ramos-Chertok

Copyright © 2018 Maria Ramos-Chertok
iMAGINe Flight Press

ISBN:10:1717104703
ISBN-13:978-1717104700

To the butterflies
whose transformation
shows us what's possible

Table of Contents

Introduction

THE IDEA FOR THIS BOOK came out of a workshop I designed called The Butterfly Series. The series is a writing and creative arts workshop for women who want to explore what's next. I came up with the inspiration to develop it because it's the workshop that I wanted to take while experiencing my own life transition. I wanted a creative way to help me through this tough and confusing time, but there was nothing I could find in my midst. I'd gone to law school and was comfortable using the linear, logical, and analytical part of my brain, but that way of thinking wasn't helping.

I also wanted to engage in life with artistry. I wanted to write and make art without it having to be for any purpose other than the act of self-expression. I was scared, but I listened to my insides and followed the signs along the way that led to my piloting a six-month workshop on transformational change.

During this same period, I looked back on several of the major decisions I'd made in life to see if I could identify patterns from the other times I'd felt uncertain about what was next. As I considered the milestones of moving across the country at eighteen, creating an individual major in college, leaving the practice of law, taking a sabbatical, working as a cowgirl, becoming an organizational development consultant to nonprofits, getting married, and having children in my forties, I began to see that I always knew what I didn't want. I experienced great clarity on the things that made me feel unhappy or boxed in or uninspired. I'd use the unease to inform my process, but because I didn't have a blue print as I embarked on change, I was self-critical and felt bad about my approach; like I was unqualified to handle my life. I had not learned to accept my free-form, organic process. Looking back, I can now see that the seed of what would emerge and lead to what was next, always sprung from the clarity of knowing what no longer served my soul.

I also reflected on the fact that every time I initiated a big life transition, people around me would ask, "What are you going to do?" "What do you want to do?" "How are you going to do that?" Those questions, while often asked out of pure curiosity, put me on the defensive and made me feel like I had to have a good answer. Saying "I don't know" made me feel like a loser. Yet, the truth is that I was willingly walking into the unknown to explore the terrain.

The good news is that I have come to embrace that process as my own. That is my way. That's how I do it. I love that about me now, but it's taken a long while to get here.

My goal in The Butterfly Series is to give participants the permission to simply be and to relieve themselves of the pressure to foresee the destination or articulate a roadmap for where they are going. I intentionally ask participants experiencing a transition not to know the answers. It's freedom. It's permission. It's being without doing. As you give yourself time to just be, you allow the answers to emerge—by listening to your inner knowledge, you become able to see the signs that will lead you to where you want or need to go next.

It doesn't sound "rational"? Good. There are plenty of rational, analytical, linear thinkers around and they'll all try to talk a good talk and encourage you to develop a plan. Plans are fine, but only when it's time for a plan. In the process of transformation, it's critical not to jump to quick fixes, but to spend time building the muscle of listening to your insides and learning to trust what's happening in your heart and gut, not just in your mind. Based on my experience, learning to trust your inner wisdom is not a skill taught in elementary school, middle school, high school, or college. It's something you have to learn on your own.

How to use this book

THIS BOOK CONSISTS OF fifty-two weeks of inquiries related to transformational change. It is organized into four sections that correspond to the phases of a butterfly's life: egg, larva, chrysalis, and taking flight. Each section has thirteen inquiries. These inquiries are designed much like the open-ended questions a life coach might ask. They are meant to be used for discovery.

You can experiment with how you want to engage with your responses. Here are some options:

- Use a freewriting technique to journal
- Sit quietly and ponder
- Take a walk and use the inquiries to anchor your thoughts
- Engage in a discussion with a trusted friend, lover, spouse, family member, spiritual advisor
- Read the inquiries before you go to bed and ask yourself to dream about them
- Engage in peer coaching with someone else in transition and take turns listening to each other reflect
- Do an art project inspired by the inquiries (collage, paint, draw, photograph, sculpt, doodle)
- Read an inquiry each morning for a week and simply notice what comes to you
- Engage in a physical expression of your responses to the inquiries through movement and/or dance
- Write a song in response to the inquiries

○ Create a poem or haiku in response to the inquiries

○ Write a play or create a theatrical piece that incorporates your responses to the inquiries

I'd recommend trying each of these and seeing what happens. There might be one or two that you are naturally drawn to and a couple others that seem off limits. Stretch yourself if you're in the mood. Overall, the main thing is a commitment to engage with yourself in some meaningful way.

In many inquiries, I've listed several questions related to the same theme. I've done this because in my experience teaching and coaching, I've learned that the same question can resonate differently for different people. Feel free to explore the question that resonates most with you. If they all do, then explore them as various dimensions of the same inquiry.

If you stay with one inquiry per week, you'll have a year's worth of exploration. In the alternative, you can open the book spontaneously to the page that calls your attention and read that. No need to begin at the beginning. Trust your own process.

I do recommend using a journal to document your journey regardless of which of the options you explore. Writing for fifteen minutes a day will help you delve into the exploration and deepen your experience. The type of writing I recommend is freewriting.

Natalie Goldberg, the author of many books on writing, suggests several techniques for this writing practice, which I summarize below:

◦ Set a timer for the specific period you will write (fifteen minutes, for example)

◦ Keep your pen moving the entire time

◦ Don't think, just let the words flow

◦ Don't worry about punctuation, spelling, or grammar

◦ No crossing out

◦ Be bold

This writing is not for publication (unless you choose it to be) so feel free to write anything you like.

Another way to use this book is to consider where you are in your transition and then go directly to the section that corresponds with what you feel you need:

EGG STAGE: to simply be, without having to know the answers

LARVA STAGE: to nurture yourself and your spirit

CHRYSALIS: to be quiet, go within, and make space for your inner voice to speak

TAKING FLIGHT: to explore something new and look for expansive ways to connect with the world around you

While the butterfly symbol is widely used as a metaphor for transformation, it seems that the focus is on the caterpillar to butterfly transition. This book spends time looking at the entire cycle, beginning with birth, and gives equal weight to each phase of development. It's important to remember that the emergence of a butterfly is the last part of the cycle and there's much that comes beforehand. Keep that in mind as you consider your own process.

The material in this book is intended as a self-guided process. While you may choose to share your thoughts and discoveries with others, please be advised that there are currently no certified facilitators of The Butterfly Series. As the designer of the six-month workshop, the author of the companion workbook, and of this book of inquiries, I want to advise you to be wary of anyone promoting themselves as a facilitator of The Butterfly Series.

Who should use this book?

MY WORK IN THE Butterfly Series is exclusively with women, both cis-gendered and female-identified. Much of what I've learned from designing and teaching the series informs this book. That said, my work as a coach includes working with both women and men (cis-gendered and male or female identified). I believe this book can be used by anyone going through a life transition of any kind, involving all kinds of issues: career, education, job, relationship, loss, love, divorce, having children, adoption, self-care, health, illness, parenting, and caretaking. Often though, one's change is not as concrete as the examples offered. Instead, it emerges as a feeling or a vague sense that something needs to change, while the specifics remain unknown. That's all fine. Anything you would put under the general category of change or transition works.

Change,
transition,
and transformation

What's the difference?

THERE ARE SO MANY words that bombard us as we think about something new and a myriad of labels that we might use to describe a process we don't understand. Beyond our own labeling, others might seek to name something for us to be helpful or to better understand it for themselves.

What follows are a few of the words that will come up as you embark on this journey of exploring what's next (change, transition, transformation) and information on how I'll use these terms.

Change

CHANGE IS DOING SOMETHING different. You change your clothes, socks, underwear. You can change the hair products you use, your toothpaste, or your diet. You might also change jobs, lovers, spouses, homes, and friends. These examples run the gamut from innocuous to life-altering. While change offers something different, it doesn't necessarily result in a corresponding internal change. While we might be seeking to create a different state to our being, making a change to our external surroundings or material objects doesn't guarantee that anything will feel different on the inside.

Often, change is a way to respond to boredom or to solve problems. In the midst of personal dissatisfaction, people are prone to turn to external changes in hopes of satisfying an internal desire or need. While this strategy might work for some, it has the likelihood of only providing temporary relief to the underlying need.

Every situation is different and everyone's circumstances have innumerable variables that impact the success of any change. For example, moving out of a toxic home environment could offer exactly what is needed. In that instance, an external change is sufficient. In another instance, by moving from one place to another you find that you have simply relocated to another toxic environment. The truism, "wherever you go, there you are," captures the crux of that quandary.

My use of the word "change" in this book will focus on any new external circumstance that leads you to experience your life in a new way. An external change may or may not help you realize any desired corresponding inner transformation you are seeking.

Transition

TRANSITION REFERS TO A process. The word implies something happening over time. While the underlying event giving rise to the transition might occur in a moment or on a memorable date (losing a loved one, losing a job, graduating school, adopting a child, ending a relationship, turning eighteen, giving birth, becoming an empty nester) the process that unfolds as one responds to the event takes place over time.

Age-related transitions are another example of undergoing a process, like moving from adolescence to adulthood or from looking youthful to looking older. If you have been through either of these, you know that there were signs along the way, often small or imperceptible to an outsider, but incremental and moving clearly towards the next stage in your development.

We are an impatient culture in the United States, especially when compared with the rest of the world where things often take more time (getting water, drying clothes, waiting in lines, making telephone calls, traveling from one location to another). In our highly technology-driven environments, we access information and answers to our questions in seconds. We expect fast results and fast service. There is an impatience that inhabits our relationship to life and that impatience does us a disservice during times of transition. Wanting speedy results or the answer now can impel us to bypass the process. In transition, the process itself is the gold.

I use the word transition to describe a process that moves at its own pace and cannot be rushed. A transition can't be seen by the eye or touched with the hand. It is an experience; an emotional and/or physical process that needs to be nurtured. We feel the impact of transitions, but sometimes not until we're on the other side of them. When we're in transition, it can seem like we're lost or out of control or confused or without a North Star. Understand, as you embark on this journey, that this feeling of being adrift is both normal and, often, necessary.

Transformation

TRANSFORMATION IS "NEVER GOING back to the way you were." It was a pivotal moment for me when one of my mentors, Robert Gass, used that definition as a barometer for a successful organizational change effort. He'd ask us to assess whether the change in the organizational culture was profound enough to prevent a return to undesirable habits and patterns of behavior?

For our exploration, the first question you will need to ask yourself is whether you are seeking to transform some aspect of your life.

Is there some aspect of your current life that is no longer serving you?

Are there behaviors you engage in that are not life-affirming?

Are there things that you need to let go of in order to move on to what's next?

If you answered "yes" to any of these, then you may be seeking to transform some aspect of your being. In transformation, you are learning to embrace what's new and to incorporate that which will serve you in your new formation. Often, that means letting go of all that is not serving you.

While we may make and experience big and small changes, only some of those result in transformation. Transformation implies that there is something on the other side. It offers an opportunity for growth. To achieve this, you will be required to identify the obstacles holding you back from fully embracing the next phase of life. The process can be unsettling, challenging, and fraught with more questions than answers. This book is about that process and how to go about it with structure and support.

Embarking on the journey

WELCOME TO THE UNKNOWN. Please come in, take off your shoes, and find a comfortable place to sit. There's no need to have anything with you like a phone or a computer or a calculator. You already have everything you need. Expect distractions and noise, expect interruptions and naysayers, expect doubt and discomfort. The good news is those things are not in charge - in fact, they're just passing through. Wave to them and smile (or frown), if you're inclined. Either way is fine, but don't invite them in to sit next to you; you're not available. You're too busy being available to yourself.

Four Stages of Transformation and Fifty-Two Weeks of Inquiries

THE PROCESS I DESIGNED tracks the stages of a butterfly's development: egg, larva, chrysalis, and taking flight. I use these visual metaphors to discuss what happens during a transformative process.

Each section begins with a brief description, followed by thirteen inquiries. These inquiries are meant to be savored, like a sweet peach in summertime. Enjoy the flavor of each week. Spend time writing about or musing over the questions as they marinate inside your soul. Pay attention to what they bring up for you. Don't rush.

Luxuriate.

Fifty-Two Weeks of Inquiries for Transformation

EGG

BEING, NOT DOING

EGG

"The egg state is the beginning of all things. This is the stage at which an idea is born but has not yet become a reality."[1]

"WE ARE BEING AS we are becoming."[2] That is the mantra for this process. There is no expectation that you do anything other than what you are doing right now, nor is there any requirement that you know where you are headed or what will happen down the line. In this stage, your purpose is to be and to explore what is happening inside you. Your job is simply to notice you – to pay attention to what you think, feel, and say. In our highly cerebral society, greater emphasis often gets placed on what one is thinking. For our purposes, I'll ask you to put as great importance on what you are feeling.

As you begin this exploration of what is next on your life journey, pay attention to your head, your heart, and your gut. Honor the information of all three as equally valid, even and especially when they are saying different things to one another!

---

[1] Sams, Jamie & Carson, David. Medicine Cards: The Discovery of Power Through the Ways of Animals, Santa Fe: Bear & Company, 1988. Page 73.

[2] Author unknown

It does not all have to make sense to the head, as sometimes the organs speak different languages or dialects. Sometimes these organs don't even agree with one another. That's fine.

Your job is to value each of their messages and to pay attention to what they say before the mind talks louder and interrupts the other two—which the mind feels entitled and privileged to do—given that the dominant culture often reinforces this behavior by legitimizing thinking over feeling.

Week 1

How is your being today?

Each session of The Butterfly Series starts with this question.

It is a chance for us to check in with ourselves and to ask the question we typically ask others, "How are you?"

The opportunity in that moment is to give the question meaning and to give our attention to both the asking and the answering: How am I? How is my being today?

Being able to be present to ourselves as we sit with the answer is the beginning of our work. Sometimes we won't know the answer immediately.

Allow yourself not to know at first and to slowly tap in to knowing.

Being able to answer the question is core to forging the path of change.

Week 2

What would it take to appreciate
your existence every day?

How do you connect
to your beating heart?

EGG

As I think about my existence, I am in awe of my heartbeat. The light, pounding rhythm combined with consciousness that make up my life. There is so much to ponder in just that, yet I so easily take it for granted.

I find myself getting bored or wanting more or noticing how unsatisfied I am.

How would your day change if you sat in wonder about existing in the here and now?

What if your work is to stay connected to where you are, while lightly holding a vision of where you want your existence to be, one not canceling out the other?

Take some time to explore your being here today. Put your hand over your heart and feel the beat.

What is the source of the life force that gives you energy?

How do you connect to it?

Week 3

What is it like just to be?

EGG

A mentor reminded me once that we are human beings, not human doings.

It struck me as obvious and important, yet I had never thought about it in quite that way. How had I missed that?

If I gauge the balance of how much time I spend on each, *doing* tips the scale. I love getting things done, it's how I define my success on a given day and how I move through the day without feeling boredom.

My challenge, particularly in times of transition, has been to be with all the feelings I'm having and pay attention to them, especially feelings fraught with confusion, overwhelm, sadness, or frustration. That's when it's been hardest for me to just be.

Try minimizing the distractions that lure you away from feeling what you need to feel. Being present with yourself and others is a practice.

How might you stay connected to each present moment to find expansiveness?

Week 4

What's at stake in the beginning?

EGG

When a butterfly lays an egg, it is a beginning.

It corresponds with the end of carrying an egg inside. For the egg, a leaf becomes its new home: so many variables, so many unknowns, so many forces at play in the larger world.

There are times when we are acutely aware we are at a beginning. In some instances, we appreciate it only in retrospect.

Sometimes the beginning announces itself as an amorphous feeling. It might appear, instead, as knowledge that something is ending or needs to end.

What's at stake in the beginning?

For me, it's being in love with what's possible, combined with a fear of the same.

How about for you?

Week 5

What is it not to know?

What is it to step into the
unknown?

EGG

There's so much pressure on getting it right. So much damn pressure. I remember announcing to my law firm that I was leaving my job after fifty weeks. I knew it was the right thing to do. That's all I knew. I had no idea what I'd do next or where I was going. Every time anyone asked me where I was going, I'd tell them I didn't know. That freaked people out. How can you leave when you have no destination?

For me, the destination was defined by freeing myself from the only thing in my life I was certain was wrong.

Sometimes change begins like that.
Sometimes you only know what you don't want.

Often, understanding what you don't want is the beginning of a journey towards what you do want.

What is it like to sit with the unknown at your side and just be?

What happens inside you as you consider this?

Week 6

What does it mean to create?

What does it mean to be created?

EGG

I wonder about all the beautiful visual art, film, and writing that I come across. What is the seed of creation? How did these ideas come into being?

One of the things I love about hearing live interviews with visual artists, filmmakers, or writers is learning about the journey they took to make the art for which they're known.

The stories are always intriguing—sometimes filled with magic and serendipity, sometimes with grit and determination, other times with clarity of vision—often with all three.

An idea, a conversation, a dream, an inspiration, a shortcoming, a misfortune.

Let your life be the petri dish for creativity.

What are you creating?

Week 7

How does your being
feel about change?

What changes are beckoning?

EGG

Some of us like change, some of us don't.

Typically, it's not an either/or—rather it depends on the kind of change involved. In my late teens and twenties, I moved eighteen times in eighteen years. I thrived on the freedom of being able to invent myself over and over. Not all the changes were great, but they were mine.

Often, though, change is forced upon us by others: displacement, eviction, and/or leaving home to escape harm.

As you look at your life and the changes you've experienced, what is your relationship to change?

What role might freedom, choice, or necessity have played?

What changes are simmering inside you?

Week 8

What comes to you in dreams/a dream state?

EGG

Lately I've been experiencing dreams as alternate realities. I feel as if I have entered a parallel plane of existence where the dream exists. This morning, in fact, I had a dream in which someone gave me a hug with such depth of emotion that it matched the most heartfelt hug I've experienced in my awake, non-dream state.

Dreams involve transitions - into and out of the dream, within the dream itself, and then back to a waking state.

How might you use dreams to receive information about your transition and feel that which is easier to access when you are not fully conscious?

How might the ease of dreaming compliment your state as a human being?

This week, before you fall asleep, ask for a dream to inform your transition.

Week 9

What is your relationship to those
who've come before you?

How might your ancestors
have imagined you?

Thinking about those who have come before you, whether in your direct ancestral line or otherwise, can be a powerful way to contextualize transition. The birth, life, death cycle is a reminder of our temporary status.

Many people and cultures feel the presence of ancestors and have a daily practice of honoring the influence and messages from those we cannot see.

Your physical being is here because of the decisions and actions of those who preceded you.

Do you ever wonder if your ancestors imagined you?

Have you imagined those to whom you will become an ancestor?

Take this week to inquire what your ancestors have to teach you about change.

Week 10

What is it to be guided
by a feeling that is not data driven
or based on hard evidence?

In law school, I studied how evidence can be used to prove that something is true. In my life, though, there are things I know and feel that are not based on research or statistics.

In fact, the most important things seem to be based on my heart. By my definition, much of what is required of us during a life change is to move into unknown territory with an uncharted route.

How might you allow yourself to embrace change without having to know the route? That doesn't mean you can't explore and research and map things out, but maybe it means you don't always have to.

Start with what you know to be true and go from there without a definite path.

What would it take for you to give yourself permission to be guided by something other than data or research? Why not give it a try?

Week 11

How do you yearn
for the unknown?

How does the yet-to-be
speak to you?

How do you
respond to the calling?

EGG

What urges do you have? I often yearn for solitude or sometimes for a smile from a passerby or sometimes for fish tacos with my grandma's homemade coleslaw. The urges just come.

I don't have to think them into existence, I just experience them as there—appearing like a leaf falling from a branch as I pass by or like an alarm going off in the distance.

It's my job just to be with them and, eventually, decide if I'm going to shrug them off or do something to make them happen.

At the beginning, though, I just have to receive.

What's calling your attention this week?

What urges are speaking to you?

Which will you honor?

Which will honor you?

Week 12

What would it take for you to feel like you are enough just as you are?

EGG

I've spent years trying to counter the messages that my breasts are too small, my thighs have too much cellulite, my arms are too hairy, I am not smart enough, I don't speak Spanish well enough...the list goes on.

What aspects of your being have been told they are not enough? How might you let go of comparing yourself to others? What would it take to appreciate your being just as it is?

As you think about your transition, I challenge you to work on the inner and not default to buying or seeking a quick fix that will move you out of the muck. External quick fixes can feel good, but they risk being temporary.

Maybe go inside this week and visit the places that need acceptance.

Week 13

How can you trust yourself?

EGG

My biggest challenge with change is that I haven't trusted myself. I feel something, but then judge it as wrong, stupid, unrealistic, impetuous, or weird.

In retrospect, every one of those times that I wanted something different—a change—my insides were right. I had no experience of me being the expert on me—there were so many others that knew better: the rules, the schools, the people with degrees. I often deferred to what I was supposed to do, what made the most sense, or the way it was supposed to look.

At those times in life when I didn't, I was happiest.

Wise counsel from others is irreplaceable, but don't forget wise counsel from yourself.

What would it be like if you trusted yourself?

What would it take?

LARVA

NOURISHMENT

LARVA

In this stage the egg hatches and a tiny caterpillar emerges. Its job is to eat from the leaf on which it is born (and then to eat some more of the same!) so that it can grow.

I'VE LEARNED SO MUCH about butterflies! One of the amazing things that I now know is that female butterflies lay their eggs on the type of leaf perfectly suited for their species of butterfly. That makes it very convenient for the larva to simply hatch and have a virtual landscape of ready-to-eat green nutrients. It can also eat the egg sac in which it's been enclosed, as that sac contains many nutrients. Aahh...what can we learn from this profound, yet simple, arrangement between mother butterfly and Mother Nature?

Here's what I'm learning:

 ◦ We each have different leaves that are just right for us and we have to find the proper leaves that will nourish us correctly.

 ◦ There is some inner knowing that mother butterflies have about what type of leaf is the proper one. They don't have to ask anyone or read about it in the newspaper – they just know.

 ◦ There are times in life when your main job is just to eat and eat and eat and grow and get strong, so you can take the next step that life has in store for you. It is always your job to nourish yourself, but there are some times in life when it's your primary, top-of-the-list, must do, urgent responsibility.

° It doesn't always have to be so hard. It may be that what you need is closer than you think or more easily accessible than you're imagining. It may be that you already have everything you need and all you have to do is be willing to nourish yourself thoroughly.

° Everyone celebrates the beauty of the butterfly. Very little is worshipped about the tiny larva as it hatches from the egg sac, begins to morph into a caterpillar, and starts eating everything in sight. We love the end product, but don't give much credence to all the work that's gone into getting there. So, don't expect much fanfare as you do what you need to do. It's not the time for recognition, and your work may be imperceptible to the naked eye.

In each session of The Butterfly Series, participants engage in activities to feed the soul and nourish the spirit. This is the proverbial "eating" that the tiny larva does.

In this section, I'll encourage you to pay attention to what "feeds" you: *What are you drawn to? What do you love? What is calling you?* The answers to these questions are the leaves upon which you should chomp, chomp, chomp.

Week 14

How do feed yourself?

How is your relationship to food
honoring your body,
or not?

LARVA

During my first year in college, I was anorexic for a period. I stopped feeling worthy of food. This was not a conscious choice, but deep inside me I sought to control something. That first year in college I lost my father to an early death, moved across the country alone, and became financially independent. Looking back, I wonder how much that huge change in my life contributed to my sense of not feeling adequate and wanting to thin myself away.

Our relationship to food and taking care of our bodies can be impacted by many things, including access to healthy food, economic resources, and messages we receive about food from our families, advertising, friends, and intimate partners.

As you move through this transition period in your life, begin to notice how you feed yourself, both literally and figuratively.

What nourishes you?

Focus on those things that will nurture your body.

Week 15

What do you crave?

What is it to
honor your hunger
for something?

How do you give yourself
permission to want?

LARVA

Take a minute to open the doors of your imagination and dream. Let the boundaries fall away and consider what you want.

Do this for as long as you like. Notice what happens.

Does a smile cross your face; do you feel energized? Does the rational, self-protecting voice of doubt begin to interrupt your fantasy?

Our wants and desires are real and they come from that magical place of inspiration.

There are a lot of things we're taught we *should* want. Check in with yourself to decipher if your wants are yours or those placed on you from external sources.

Keep it simple to begin with. You may want a bouquet of flowers near your bedside.

Start with something easy and then deepen the listening to your insides.

Begin to take note of your desires and treat them as precious, delicate treasures.

Week 16

What is it like to imagine
a cornucopia of options?

LARVA

In the book *Creative Visualization*, Shakti Gawain introduces a cornucopia meditation. Imagining a cornucopia has always been hard for me because I don't like waste and have spent much of my life getting by paycheck to paycheck.

Living beyond the bare necessities had not been my experience. Yet, I realize that I was scared to even imagine an abundance of beauty or an abundance of joy.

My unwillingness to give myself a moment of imaginary fun was part of my self-denial and of my deep fear that I would never know this state of satiation.

This imagining is not meant to deny the realities of economic hardship that many face, nor is it intended to curb your quest for worldwide justice.

Instead, it is meant to inform and expand your capacity to imagine and open your mind to the possibility of abundance, for you and for every being.

Go for it.

Imagine.

Week 17

What messages
about self-nourishment/care
have you internalized?

How do you push away the voices
that say,
"selfish,"
"greedy,"
"undeserving,"
"privileged,"
"entitled,"
"bourgeois"?

Many of us have internalized the notion that taking care of self is something that only those with class privilege can afford. There are realities about inequitable access to money and leisure time.

Within those real constraints, though, are also internalized messages that many women carry about caretaking.

There are both societal and cultural pressures put upon women to attend to the needs of others in order to be "good" mothers, wives, partners, lovers, daughters, daughters-in-law, sisters, and granddaughters.

What are the critical words that enter your head when you think about or act on self-care? What words are you using to distance yourself from attending to your needs? What are the messages you receive when you attend to self?

What must move out of the way so that you can give attention to you?

Week 18

How might self-care be
an act of resistance?

How might care for others
be rooted in care for self?

LARVA

Audre Lorde said, "Caring for myself is not self-indulgence, it is self-preservation, and that is an act of political warfare."

In discussing this quote, a dear friend recently asked me, "What if we didn't have to be at war in order to take care of ourselves?" I resisted her query. But we, as women and people of color, are at war, I thought. Yet, I am sitting with her question.

To what extent have I accepted a military mentality about my survival?

What if we took care of ourselves, just because?

What if our ability to care for others was deeply connected to understanding what self-care is and how it feels?

Moving through transition can be stressful.

What do you need to understand in order to care, or better care, for you? What would it be like if we weren't at war?

Allow yourself to imagine peace as a must-have as you care for your soul.

Week 19

Who/what nourishes you?

What sustains you?

Where do you get
the energy to go on?

The act of nourishment is profound in its necessity. Without feeding our bodies, we become frail and ultimately perish. Feeding is a precondition of life.

Think about the ways you nourish your body. What promotes your health?

There's also the question of how you feed your soul. That might be less obvious to you. Or, you may be feeding your soul well and not feeding your body well.

Notice if there is an imbalance or void in one or the other.

What and who give you that feeling of aliveness? Excitement? What gives you the good jitters? Pay attention to those moments when you feel your spirit jolt awake.

Consider, too, what calms your soul and helps you feel grounded.

This week, become a keen observer of the sources of your nourishment.

Week 20

Who/what doesn't sustain and nourish you?

LARVA

Where might you be stressing your system with things that are not keeping you healthy?

We all know what habits we have that don't contribute to our well-being. We all know those people in our lives that don't lift us up.

I've gone through periods where I've had to do an actual "spring cleaning" of people from my life. There were people trying to control me.

There were others who took up too much space in our interactions and got used to me being the giver, the listener, the attentive one.

I hid behind this convenience because it meant I didn't have to talk about myself.

Over time, though, I found I was disappearing. I had no one to listen to me and didn't feel seen in many of my friendships. That's *my* story of identifying what was unsustainable.

What's yours?

Week 21

How might you flourish with fear?

What would it take for you
to thrive?

LARVA

During times of transition, it is easy to get unmoored—to sense that there's nothing to ground you.

We feel constricted and fearful; we have questions without answers. We spend many hours feeling lost.

What would it be like to connect to your aliveness when these moments take you over?

How about inviting it all to coexist: the questions, the fear, and the instability, along with your beating heart. Is there any way to thrive in the darkness of not knowing what's next?

Can you feed yourself life tonic and do something this week that enlivens you?

Even as you feel lost—especially because you feel lost.

How might you thrive in the fact that you're alive?

Week 22

Who cares for you?

LARVA

I can easily make a list of those I care for.

Go ahead and take a moment to create a mental list of who you care for.

Now, I want you to make a list of those who care for you.

Write this one down in your journal or on a piece of paper. There may be crossover of the lists. That's fine. Who loves you? Who takes time to listen to you? Who spends time with you in ways that feel supportive? Who has your back? Who helps you get things done?

I feel it's important to say that if anyone on your "Cares for Me" list is also abusing you in any way—that's not care.

Look over your list.

Have you told each person on your list how much their care means to you? Please do.

Write a note, send a card, have a talk.

Honor the care you receive.

Week 23

How do you encourage
laughter in your life?

LARVA

During times of transition, it's especially important to laugh. We become serious or fearful or focused, and it's easy to forget we have one simple, affordable, accessible tool at our disposal.

I use a laughter-scale to let me know how I'm doing. If I go through long periods of time without a belly laugh—that's not good for me.

This is not to be confused with laughing at yourself. There's time for that when things get too heavy, but what I'm talking about here is pure, happy laughter.

What are the situations you find joy-full? Who are the people you can crack up with? What movie has you laughing the hardest?

Go find them and engage in the best medicine available.

Week 24

What is the recipe of you?

What ingredients make up your being?

LARVA

In my workshops I ask participants to write about their lives as a recipe.

What ingredients are you made of?

What gets thrown into the pot and in what quantity? Do you add spices? What kind? Do you stir, blend, use a mortar and pestle? Are you grinding corn or acorns with black stones? Are you using a clay pot?

How is your being put together?

What role do your ancestors play in the recipe of you?

Might you add flowers? Mountains? Rivers? Animals? Continents? Galaxies?

Let your imagination bring together the ingredients and the instructions on preparation. You may even begin a family recipe book.

Have fun!

Week 25

Where do you lose track of time?

What are the places
where you are
in the zone,
the flow,
the harmony?

I know I'm doing something l love when I lose track of time. I've had jobs where I regularly checked the clock and celebrated the passage of fifteen minutes. My obsession with the passage of time drained my energy.

Whether it's paid work or time away from the job, think about those situations in which time flows and you are in the zone. What situations energize you?

Who are you with? What are you doing?
What is the environment?

Cherish the answers.

Is there a way to bring that harmony into your life more?

What would have to change in order for it to happen?

Take your next smallest step in that direction this week.

Week 26

What's calling your attention?

What do you notice?

Where are you drawn in?

LARVA

It's important during transition to notice what you are attracted to. There are messages in where your attention leads you.

Honor those things calling out to you. It may be a subject you're curious about. It may be a name that pops into your head. It may be a book you are drawn to. It may be a color. It may be a country.

Your inner self is attuned to what's needed in ways the rational brain may not recognize.

As the poet Rumi states, "Let yourself be silently drawn by the strange pull of what you really love. It will not lead you astray."

How might paying attention to what calls your attention inform the journey you are on?

CHRYSALIS

THE POWER OF STILLNESS

CHRYSALIS

In this stage the caterpillar creates a chrysalis around itself. In this self-made enclosure, the next stage of transformation can occur. It is not a resting period – in fact much is happening. While to the outside observer things appear static, inside a butterfly is being created.

I FIND GREAT COMFORT in the miracle of the chrysalis stage. It is a time for the caterpillar to become what's next. It is not appearing as a butterfly, nor is it one. Yet, in order for a butterfly to ultimately emerge, this inner time must exist. This period is quiet, yet not necessarily restful. A lot is happening.

The other thing I so appreciate is that there does not appear to be a lot of rational analysis in this stage – just an innate sense of timing that is driven by what I'll call "nature." Does the caterpillar even have a choice as to whether or not to honor its nature? I suspect not. This is simply what is required at this time in its life cycle. This stage teaches us that there may be a time during transformation when what's required is for us to simply go within. From the outside, it might not look like much is happening. Those who want to track our success by measurable results may be disappointed. Our inner critic might also be dismissive of an internal process and plague us with the question, "What are you doing?" Your response: "I'm being."

There's another question that can arise in connection with a desire to be more internal for a period: How do I know I am in process and not simply hiding out, avoiding the hard stuff and/or failing to take advantage of the opportunities around me that would help me get to the next place?

Answer: You don't. But if you are paying attention to what's going on within you - really listening to you - you'll know the difference between hiding out or avoidance and simply giving yourself time to be.

Quieting the mind and not doing anything can be a powerful tool in transformation. In the following inquiries, you will spend time going within. That will take different forms depending on your preference. It might be via a silent sitting meditation, a guided visualization and/or a walking meditation. Other ways to access the stillness can be through writing, walking, day dreaming, artistic expression, and tracking your night time dreams. All of these tap into a type of powerful inner stillness reminiscent of the chrysalis.

Week 27

What is it like just to be still?

Many people have a difficult relationship to stillness. They associate stillness with boredom. Children are often scolded to sit still, when it may be that stillness is not what their bodies need at the moment.

There is both the sought after, desirable form of physical stillness and the imposed physical stillness resulting from injury or infirmity.

Beyond the physical, though, lies the stillness of the mind and the stillness of the soul.

How would you describe your relationship to physical stillness? Mental stillness?
Stillness of your soul?

Are you satisfied with these relationships?

If so, amazing.

If not, what needs to happen to increase your comfort and delight with stillness?

Week 28

What happens as you listen
to the sound of the breeze
swishing past the leaves?

What happens when
there are no leaves and
it's just the sound of swirling air?

What happens when you listen?

CHRYSALIS

I've often been in homes where the television, stereo, or radio is always on. Some folks like to have music on everywhere they go. These days it's easy to be connected to sound 24/7.

This week, try to unplug and listen to the sound of the wind, or the sounds of the breeze in the leaves.

If you are in an urban environment, make your way to a park or focus on big city noises: horns, sirens, buses, the underground, snippets of conversation.

Sometimes there's poetry in the sounds around us.

Can you tap into your environment with more observation and begin noticing what happens when you are still and listening, even when everything around you isn't?

What have you been missing?

Week 29

What is your gut
telling you about transformation?

What are your insides saying?

How do you make space
for the inner sound of your
wisdom?

CHRYSALIS

I often ask people where they feel their intuition. How do they know when their intuition is speaking? Some point to their gut and talk about a sensation, a sense of knowing.

There are numerous other ways the intuition makes itself known.

How does it show up for you? What is your inner wisdom saying about the current transition you are in?

Ask it.

What might be needed for transformation to occur?

Ask again.

How are you making space for these messages to be heard? What has worked in the past? What do you need to do more or less of in order for your inner knowing to have the space to emerge?

Week 30

How do you sit with yourself?

CHRYSALIS

There are people who are always in relationships and who've never had the opportunity to live on their own or spend a length of time by themselves.

I value community and I understand how important community is to my life, my identity, and my happiness. That said, there may be value during transition to commune with yourself.

Find time to be with yourself, away from others.

Maybe taking a walk, maybe sitting in a temple, ashram, church, synagogue, monastery, or mosque. Maybe find a quiet bench in a park or on a mountain top. Maybe take yourself on a date.

Consider the current balance in your life and ask yourself if the balance feels right.

If it doesn't, consider what you might do differently to rebalance the scale to make time to be alone with yourself.

Week 31

What type of enclosure
might feel nurturing to you?

What does your chrysalis look
like?

CHRYSALIS

I have a shawl that belonged to my stepmother.

She asked that it be gifted to me after her death. I keep it on my desk chair and look at it every day. I don't always tap into the significance of it; sometimes I just see it.

Other days I talk to it and talk to her through it. When I wrap myself in it, the deep browns and aquas hold me and keep me warm.

I treasure this protection she thought of leaving for me because it's her way of hugging me even though she's not here. I feel nurtured when it's on.

What are the things or places that nurture you?

Where do you feel a sense of peace?

Find your chrysalis.

Week 32

What role might alcohol or drugs play in keeping you from yourself?

CHRYSALIS

How Are you using drugs and/or alcohol, if at all, and to what end?

At different times in my life, I've used both to create a sense of excitement or to cut the stress in a situation or to deal with something that was soul-crushing.

The year I spent working as a corporate attorney was the year I learned how much I looked forward to a vodka and grapefruit juice after work. It became the highlight of my day. The alcohol kept me distracted from my unhappiness.

What is your relationship to drugs and/or alcohol and what role do they play in your transition?

What needs to shift?

Be honest. Indulge yourself in truth.

Week 33

How might you be with others
in silence?

How might you invite others
to be in silence with you?

CHRYSALIS

A friend told me a story of being hospitalized. During his stay, many people came to visit, but the one that he remembers the most is the one who came to his bedside and kept him company. Essentially, just sat with him.

There was no expectation of conversation, no desire to entertain, no pressure for my friend to be awake or asleep. When my friend dozed off, he would wake to find this person sitting there quietly by his side. Sometimes this person would read to my friend for a bit, but often he did nothing in particular.

As you might have guessed, this was before the self-entertaining role of cell phones. My friend told me this was the most helpful person throughout his entire recovery.

I marvel at that, because my visits to friends and family in hospitals or rehabilitation centers have always been meant to entertain and engage. I never imagined simply being company with no larger purpose.

How might you engage with others during your transition based on what you need versus what they want to give you?

How might the company of silence soothe your soul?

Week 34

What's brewing inside you?

CHRYSALIS

People often tell me that they can feel something brewing inside that portends change. This "something" can be hard to describe. They often have a vague sense of it, sometimes a strong sense of it.

People seek confirmation from me that they are still a legitimate candidate for The Butterfly Series even though they can't articulate what the change is or where they are going. I assure them that the series was designed with them in mind.

Our bodies and souls often know things before our minds do. That feeling inside is a key indicator of something important to pay attention to.

If you tell me, "I've got a feeling..." then I'll assure you, you've come to the right place.

Pay attention to what's brewing inside you.

Sometimes you feel before you know.

What's that feeling inside you saying?

Week 35

Looking back on changes
you've made in the past,
what role did
stillness/
quiet/
inactivity play?

CHRYSALIS

When I look back on my life and some of the changes I've made, I recognize how often my impatience was the driving force in choosing to act. I got tired of waiting for an answer or got over-whelmed by the confusion I felt. I wanted answers.

Another aspect of this is rushing. Many of the biggest messes I've gotten into were due to me rushing: pulling out of the garage with the garage door closed; rushing up a mountain on a hike and falling and bashing my leg; hurrying to work and colliding with the oncoming car on the other side of the small hill.

When I find myself rushing these days, I try to interrupt it.

As you look back on your life, what role has stillness, quiet, or inactivity played or conversely, what role has impetuousness played?

What can be learned here regarding your transition?

Week 36

What's on the brink for you?

CHRYSALIS

The brink is a crucial point.

When the butterfly is in its chrysalis, it's on the brink of something magical—it's that period before the emergence, before the birth, before the new state comes into being. It's a time ripe with possibility.

It's also a time where lots of energy has to converge to shepherd in the new.

From the outside, though, it may look like nothing is happening.

Our society gets caught up in appearances—looking good, sometimes by any means necessary and at any cost.

Maybe this is a time in your transition to go within and stop putting effort into your outer looks. You are on the brink.

What on the inside needs attending to in order to give birth to what's next?

Week 37

What growth and preparation
are needed so that
you can emerge?

It's not necessarily easy going as you're preparing for what's next.

We want the outcome, but sometimes we need new skills or tools or information to ensure that we're prepared to take on the next challenge. Learning a language, a skill, a new way of treating people all require work.

Don't be afraid to do an honest assessment of what skills you have that are helpful to you now and what things you need to learn in order to feel confident that you're closer to being ready for what's next.

Maybe what's needed is a new relationship with yourself.

Take inventory and then take action.

Week 38

What are you resisting?

When I was being trained as an organizational development consultant, one of my teachers said that when we encounter resistance on the part of a client, think of it as a friend. It took me a while to understand what that meant. In hindsight, it's become one of the most useful lessons I have learned.

Resistance indicates that place where we bump up against fear and uncertainty.

It presents as an obstacle, when it's really a wellspring of information.

What are you hesitant about? What additional information would you need to take the next step?

What support could I provide to assist you in feeling confident that we were moving in the right direction?

These are examples of the types of questions I'd ask a client.

Why not try asking these questions to yourself in those places in your transition where you come up against resistance?

Week 39

When might lusting
after a specific outcome
circumvent your inner knowing?

How might certainty be
too convenient?

CHRYSALIS

We want certainty.

We want a guarantee that what we're contemplating or envisioning is correct. What I know for sure is that certainty does not always serve me well.

I remember meeting someone in my mid-thirties who I was sure was the one—absolutely certain. After six months we moved in together, and six months after that I was a wreck of a person, not able to think my way out of a paper bag. The relationship was a disaster.

Once we saw each other's vulnerabilities and flaws, we both fell into a deep pit of disillusionment and didn't have the ability to work our way out of it. I moved out. It took me two years to regain my emotional stability, but I did and then I actually met someone who I took time to get to know. That served me better.

I wish I didn't have to go through the emotional torment of the previous relationship, but that was part of a process that helped me get ready for meeting the real one.

Where might certainty be shortchanging your process?

TAKING FLIGHT

A NEW PERSPECTIVE

EMERGE AND TAKE FLIGHT

In this stage, the butterfly emerges. Its wings are wet. It has to pump blood into them to get them fully extended and ready for flight.

THE INQUIRIES IN THIS section ask you to think about "flight." Taking flight is often a big moment of faith. The opportunity to take flight is a launch out into the world anew. You're being asked to consider where you want to "pump blood." This is another way of asking, "As you honor your transition, what needs your attention?" What steps might you take to prepare for flight?

Take some time to think about what you'd like to muse on, do, explore, attempt or with whom you'd like to connect, play or network.

You'll also want to consider how you will hold yourself accountable for the steps you commit to take. Do you need to engage the help of a coach or thought partner? Do you want to engage in peer coaching? Do you want to join a group or put together a group of other people in transition?

Give some thought to what type of support would be useful.

Week 40

What might it be like to welcome flight?

TAKING FLIGHT

Up until this point, the butterfly has known life primarily on land: leaves, branches, and suspension in a chrysalis, none of which compares to flight.

Imagine emerging from a chrysalis with lovely wings that you have to pump full of life in order to take flight.

You are presented with an opportunity to explore the world in a new way, with a new purpose, part of which is to help pollinate flowers.

A completely new reality with a new vista point awaits.

Where in your own transition do you have a new vantage point? What can you see from it that you could not see before?

What newfound freedom exists as you set forth?

What beauty are you helping create by taking flight?

Week 41

What might you have
to let go of in order to
move forward?

TAKING FLIGHT

Taking flight necessarily means leaving behind the trusted way of doing things. In gaining wings, the caterpillar is leaving behind undulating locomotion—essentially all that it knew about how to get around.

The metamorphosis has a life of its own that propels the caterpillar into what's next.

For me, choosing to get married and have a family at forty scared me because it meant leaving behind the many ways I walked in the world as a single person. I understood I would not have the freedom to do it all my way, every day.

This was a cause for concern, but I let it go and that helped move me into what was awaiting me as a partner and mother.

As you consider taking flight, what will you have to let go of?

What will you leave behind?

What could assist you to move into the next phase of life with ease?

Week 42

What can you commit to?

What's easy?

What's the low-hanging fruit?

How can you set yourself up
for success?

TAKING FLIGHT

It doesn't always have to be so hard. Sometimes it will be. That's reality. And, there may be times when it doesn't have to be.

I got used to everything in life being hard and I couldn't imagine it not being so. Yet, over time, I found that sometimes I talked myself into a frenzy when the situation did not require it.

I now look for ways to set myself up for success. I'll begin with two minutes each morning of stretching to alleviate my back pain instead of twenty. I'll sit quietly for six minutes in the morning instead of thirty. I'll do a free write for fifteen minutes, not twenty-five, and see how I feel after that. I want to be on my side and I have to be very conscious about it.

How can you set yourself up for success as you take flight?

What's easy?

Begin there.

Week 43

How do you follow the signposts?

How do you
let the breadcrumbs
lead you on your journey?

In The Butterfly Series, I call signs that appear to show you the way, "breadcrumbs." I tell participants to "follow the breadcrumbs."

There are all kinds of ways for breadcrumbs to manifest. When I was piloting my first workshop, I was trying to figure out who to invite. As I was sitting at my desk contemplating this, a name popped into my head. At first I couldn't even remember how I knew the woman, although the name was familiar to me. I ended up calling her and telling her about the project and she became one of the six women to participate. We hadn't spoken or seen one another in several years. She was a colleague, not someone I knew well. It doesn't have to make sense to you how this works.

All you have to do is pay attention to what appears.

How are the breadcrumbs being revealed? Where is serendipity showing up?

How are you doing following the clues?

Week 44

What do you know to be true?

TAKING FLIGHT

As you take flight, there are apt to be things about which you are unsure.

No problem. Just ground yourself in what you know to be true.

As I was leaving a high-paying corporate job, I had no idea what was next, but I was sure I was going to find work that was meaningful. I knew I would stop having that drink after work. I knew I was not going to make money my highest priority. And I knew I could do without most of the things that created "golden handcuffs" for my colleagues. I knew I'd be willing to live without a car. I knew I'd live with roommates. I knew I didn't need expensive clothing or jewelry. I knew thrift stores were fine for me.

This doesn't mean these things have to be true for you—I'm just giving you my list.

These core truths helped guide me as I made decisions.

As you take flight, what do you know for certain?
Use core principles to ground you in who you are becoming.

Week 45

Who do you
have to forgive
in order to fully step
into what's next?

From whom
must you ask forgiveness
in order to fully step
into what's next?

TAKING FLIGHT

Forgiveness is big.

Often you will have to seek forgiveness from yourself. When I was attempting to regain my center after a difficult break-up, one of the hardest parts was forgiving myself for making such a wrong decision and for allowing myself to fall for someone who wasn't able to love me in a way that felt supportive.

I was mad at myself, I blamed myself, and I felt I could never trust me again. In order to really move on and take flight, I had to forgive. It was hard.

At this point in your transition, who do you need to forgive in order to move on?

Who will you decide not to forgive? That's an option too, as long as it serves you well.

From whom might you ask for forgiveness so that you can be emotionally, mentally, and/or spiritually released to take flight?

Week 46

Who are you becoming?

What is on your horizon?

Visioning is important. It is the ability to imagine that which has yet to take form.

It's an interesting endeavor to use creativity to develop a picture of what you want to manifest. It's like a mental work of art.

Once it exists on the mental plane, the next step is to articulate it.

Tell people what your vision is. Write about your vision. Create vision boards. Draw your vison. Do a spoken word performance about your vision. Write slam poetry about your vision.

Each step you take to bring it into the world creates unseen ripples of energy that interact with other hearts and minds and allow great things to happen.

You can't write the script for this part; your job is simply to put it out there in the world and love it, believe in it, and commit to it.

What is your vison for taking flight?

Be bold.

Week 47

Who might you be
talking to and meeting with
to help you
get to what's next?

TAKING FLIGHT

It may feel that lots of your transition has been spent alone. In the muck, in the uncertain, in the gray...just splashing around in the mud.

That's certainly part of it, but when you are taking flight it's time to reach out.

Think about those people you know who are doing what you want to be doing or who have a skill you want to learn or who live a lifestyle you aspire to. Write them, call them, invite them to tea or over for homemade scones.

This isn't the time for shyness. You'll have to be bold. If you don't know how - figure it out. Try something. Don't hold back. What's the worst they can say? NO? So what? Ask someone else. Have a long list and go down it one by one. This is the time to be methodical. Ask each person you talk to, "who else should I be talking to?"

If you want to take flight, you need wings and these folks make up a piece of your wings. Go for it and be curious about what you can learn.

Adopt the mindset of a private investigator seeking the clues to solve the puzzle.

Week 48

Who can support your boldness?

Who can be a midwife
for your fear?

TAKING FLIGHT

As you are taking flight, surround yourself with people who believe in you. If you don't have any of them around, sit down and call upon a guardian angel.

Imagine what qualities this protector would have and summon them to guide you. If this doesn't feel right, summon something that does. It doesn't matter what you call it—just that you access a source of support.

When I was giving birth to my son, my pregnancy was deemed high risk because I was forty years old. When my water broke I went to the hospital. They wanted to keep me there—in bed, strapped to monitors. I wasn't even close to two centimeters dilated. I wanted to go home and walk around. The doctor told me I would be endangering the health of my child if I left. Then a nurse walked into the room and whispered in my ear that I could ask for an injection of antibiotics that would keep the baby safe from infection for a week. I did and I left. That nurse was my guardian of boldness. She appeared when I needed her. My baby was fine; I was fine.

Summon the people who can support your boldness. What qualities would they have? What information might they provide?

Week 49

How might your boldness
impact the others around you?

TAKING FLIGHT

Your boldness may scare others. Don't take on their fears.

Your willingness to fly may magnify the static state of those around you.

When I was embarking on a six-month journey by myself throughout Mexico, the southwest of the U.S., and Canada, people I barely knew started telling me stories about solo travelers being killed or abducted. I began having nightmares because I internalized their fears.

I went on the trip anyway and it was one of the most transformative experiences of my life.

I took precautions and limited my risk by using good judgment, but I didn't let my fears prevent me from taking flight.

What are the people in your orbit saying as you begin to take flight? How might your boldness be a threat to them?

Watch, look, and listen, but don't let it stop you from soaring.

Week 50

What role does fear play
in taking flight?

TAKING FLIGHT

Lately, I've been astonished as I uncover the various ways that fear spreads its tentacles into my being. I fear someone not liking me. I fear being bored. I fear not being a good enough mother. I fear not having the drive I should. I fear that I'm spending too much time alone. I fear that my writing isn't good enough.

Shall I go on? Let's just sum it up by saying fear permeates my being in ways of which I'm usually not even conscious. I really have to stop and shine a spotlight on my insides in order to find fear peeking its head around the corner.

Everyone has fears; it's a perfectly normal response to being alive and observant. And, fear can't be the driver. You have to grab the steering wheel and take over the course of your journey.

Make a list of all your fears and just notice them. They don't define you. They just are.

Take flight and if your fear wants to come along, tell it to sit in the back seat and buckle up for the ride.

Week 51

What do you love?

TAKING FLIGHT

In essence, taking flight is about love. Loving yourself enough to listen and to believe in what you feel. Being pulled by the draw of what you love into becoming whatever is next. This will happen over and over.

If you are being guided by love, there's no stopping deep transformation because you are constantly becoming—you are never static, even when it feels like you are.

Once I was working with a client, and I didn't feel my coaching was going well. I checked in with a mentor about it and his first and only question to me was, "Do you love her?" I was stopped in my tracks. Love? I wasn't even sure I liked her. His response was simple. "If you don't love her, you shouldn't be working with her."

That was a transformative moment for me and I understood then, why I didn't feel effective. I need to put my attention and intention towards love.

Anything else is a waste. Take note.

What is it that you love? How might you be guided by that as you take flight?

Week 52

What's after flight?

TAKING FLIGHT

When you get to that moment of flight, feeling at one with the wind, being carried lightly to do what you are being called to do, there is a responsibility.

I believe the opportunity exists to reach out and provide support to someone else who needs to be reminded of their greatness. It really helps when someone can see greatness in another when that person can't access it themself.

Hold that person to the highest standard of what they can be. Be an unabashed cheerleader—it can't be fake— you have to really feel it.

Offer a hand. Lend an ear. Provide a shoulder. Give a ride. Write a letter. Make the call. Fix something broken. Buy a gift. Cook a meal. Give a bed.

Do whatever it is you can do. It doesn't have to cost money—it just has to be what the person wants, which might be different from what you think they need. Be able to distinguish between the two. Ask if you don't know. Listen deeply. Know that your presence can make a difference.

Do this over and over until everyone in your orbit has felt the magic of your presence.

Again and Again

You will go through many transitions in life and likely will support others as they, too, experience life's constant cycle of birth, decay, death, and renewal.

At the crux of it all, is the challenge to be present to yourself and those around you so that you can face each moment with awareness and, ideally, an open heart.

May this book be a gift to support you.

May you find comfort and solace.

May you find joy.

May you learn to love each step of your gift of life.

Additional Reading

Bridges, William. Managing Transitions: Making the Most of Change 4th edition, Reading: Perseus Books, 2016.

Johnson M.D., Spencer. Who Moved My Cheese? An A-Mazing Way to Deal with Change in Your Work and in Your Life, New York: G.P. Putnam's Sons, 1998.

Lawrence-Lightfoot, Sara. The Third Chapter: Passion, Risk, and Adventure in the 25 Years After 50, New York: Farrar, Straus and Giroux, 2009.

Paulus, Trina. Hope for the Flowers: A parable about life, revolution, hope, caterpillars, and butterflies, Mahwah: Paulist Press, 1972.

Paula, Trina. Esperanza para las Flores: Un cuento sobre la vida, revolución, esperanza, orugas, y mariposas, Mahwah: Paulist Press, 1992.

Salerno, Ann and Brock, Lillie. The Change Cycle: How People Can Survive and Thrive in Organizational Change, San Francisco: Berrett-Koehler Publishers, Inc., 2008.

Acknowledgments

Thank you to all the women who have participated in The Butterfly Series workshops and who have trusted the process.

My appreciation to Dr. Cio Hernandez for giving me the push to get this book ready and to Moxie Road Productions for guidance and support. For use of the butterfly icons, thank you to Freepik and www.flaticon.com.

Immense gratitude for my second pair of eyes, Gerard. Thank you to Tram for the first and second read. Deepest appreciation to my sister, Sandra, who read this book and handled it as if it were a precious gem. What a gift you are in my life.

Thank you to Akaya Windwood for inviting me to join the training team of Rockwood Leadership Institute in 2007. Rockwood's practices have broadened and deepened my understanding of transformation.

Heartfelt gratitude for my husband, Keith, and two sons, Joshua and Michael, for always supporting my journey and filling it with love.

About the Author

MARIA RAMOS-CHERTOK HAS worked for over twenty years as an organizational development consul-tant, coach, and trainer. She is the founder and facilitator of The Butterfly Series, a writing and creative arts workshop she designed for women who want to explore what's next. To learn more about the series, visit: www.thebutterflyseries.com.

Maria received her undergraduate degree from the University of California at Berkeley and her law degree from the University of Pennsylvania School of Law. She received coaching training from the Coaches Training Institute and spent many years learning about mediation with the Center for Understanding Conflict. She is certified in Interpersonal Leadership Styles (ILS), a powerful interpersonal communications tool that focuses on individual styles of behavior and the impact different styles have on the quality of relationships.

Maria is part of the training team of Rockwood Leadership Institute, where she co-leads leadership trainings for social justice change agents. For more information visit: www.mariaramoschertok.com

Maria can be found on social media, but also in real life, evolving into whatever the world has in store for her next.

17806302R00095

Made in the USA
San Bernardino, CA
19 December 2018